HEALING DELIVERANCE

Freedom from the Bondage of Satan

Volume 6
in the Healing Series

By Prince Handley

University of Excellence Press

Copyright © 2013 by Prince Handley
All Rights Reserved.

UNIVERSITY OF EXCELLENCE PRESS
Los Angeles ■ London ■ Tel Aviv

ISBN-13: 978-0692228005
ISBN-10: 0692228004

Printed in the U.S.A.

Second Edition

TABLE OF CONTENTS

INTRODUCTION

Deliverance belongs to you. To "deliver" is to "set free." Yeshua (Jesus) said, *"You shall know the truth, and the truth shall make you free"* (John 8:32).

If you know Jesus the Messiah as your Lord, **NO** demon, **NO** evil spirit can have you! Jesus said, *"If the Son therefore shall make you free, you shall be free indeed."* The Greek word here used for "indeed" (ontos) means "really, actually."

The devil (Satan) wants to hurt you and place you in bondage through various means -- even people. After that, he will **try to keep you** in bondage. God's Son, Jesus, wants to deliver you, to heal you and to make you whole.

God sent his Son, Yeshua, to earth to defeat Satan and to heal the separation between God and man. You can be **permanently delivered** from the bondage of Satan and be healed in body, mind, and spirit.

This book will teach you **how to be delivered** from the devil and his dark works.

Baruch haba b'Shem Adonai

Prince Handley

HEALING DELIVERANCE

Freedom from the Bondage of Satan

DELIVERANCE FROM
THE BONDAGE OF SATAN

There are several examples of the practice of, and the provisionary promise for, deliverance in the Holy Bible, in the lives of:

- ✓ Jesus,

- ✓ Paul and the apostles,

- ✓ Christians today.

The reader may be familiar with these, but for those people that aren't, I will describe some of them briefly here:

✓ JESUS

"Then was brought unto Him one possessed with a devil, blind, and dumb [speechless]: and He healed him, insomuch that the blind and dumb both was then able to speak and see." [Matthew 12:22]

In this case the combined conditions of being blind and dumb were probably the result of an evil spirit of affliction, as we know from this passage that the man had been possessed with a demon.

Even in a Christian's life, although a demon is NOT possessing them - Christ is possessing them - there might be a case of a spirit of sickness afflicting them. Not in all cases, but in some cases! And the spirit can be dealt with successfully in the name of Jesus, thereby effecting their deliverance and resultant healing.

"And Jesus rebuked the devil: and the demoniac being departed out of him: and the child was cured from that very hour." [Matthew 17:18]

✓ PAUL AND THE APOSTLES

"And it came to pass, as we went to prayer, a certain damsel possessed with a spirit of divination met us, which brought her masters much gain by soothsaying:

The same followed Paul and us, and cried out, saying, These men are the servants of the most high God, which show unto us the way of salvation.

And this she did many days. But Paul, being grieved, turned and said to the spirit, I command you in the name of Jesus Christ to come out of her. And he came out the same hour." [Acts 16:16-18]

"And God worked special miracles by the hands of Paul: so that from his body were brought unto the sick handkerchiefs or aprons, and the diseases departed from them, and the evil spirits went out from them." [Acts 19:11-12]

NOTE: An afflicting spirit may be sent for other reasons than those examples above. It may have an assignment from the enemy to cause fear, a false sense of inferiority, or a lack of believing for success. It may be some SEEMINGLY SMALL stronghold that has kept the Christian from excelling, succeeding, or being productive over the years . . . or entrapped in a practice.

✓ **CHRISTIANS TODAY**

"And these signs shall follow THEM THAT BELIEVE, In My name shall they cast out demonic beings, they shall speak with new tongues . . ." [Mark 16:17]

CAUSES OF SATANIC BONDAGE

There are many reasons for – or causes of – Satanic bondage:

- Involvement in witchcraft … even so-called "good" or "white" witchcraft … or wicca.

- Involvement in the occult.

- Involvement with psychic phenomena such as tarot cards, ouija boards, séances.

- Involvement with New Age or Eastern meditation.

- Involvement in religious or other cults.

- Involvement in false religions.

- Sexual perversion.

- Lies and habitual deceit.

- Pride

- Ancestral inheritance

- Sexual encounters with a demonic person

However, there CAN be **other** symptoms which can be "signs" or "manifestations" showing "borderline" cases needing deliverance. Such symptoms can be:

- Fear;

- Failure;

- Poverty,

- Sickness;

- Sins of the flesh;

- Low self esteem;

- Lack of confidence;

- Negative relationships;

- Self-defeating mentality;

- Lack of a visionary future.

In some cases, deliverance is necessary for "borderline" cases described above. However, most people overcome all of the above "borderline" cases simply by learning WHO they are and WHAT they have as a Christian.

These are learned by daily study of the Word of God and by instruction from anointed teachers of the Word. This is another reason we need to be diligent in discipling new believers: to guide them into all the resources available to them in their NEW inheritance.

HEALING DELIVERANCE FROM
THE BONDAGE OF SATAN

Deliverance belongs to you! To "deliver" is to "set free." Yeshua (Jesus) said, "And you shall know the truth, and the truth shall make you free" (John 8:32).

If you know Messiah Yeshua as your LORD, NO demon, NO evil spirit can have you! Jesus said, "If the Son therefore shall make you free, you shall be free indeed." The Greek word here used for "indeed" (ontos) means "really, actually."

If you will study the Word of God, you will KNOW that Yeshua has set you FREE, and the devil cannot have you! Resist the devil with the

Word of God. Speak God's Word to him and he will run away from you (James 4:7 in the New testament). To obtain FREEDOM in Messiah is to obtain freedom from Satan and all his demon spirits!

You shall be FREE indeed.

Ask yourself the following questions and be honest:

1. Is Messiah Yeshua (Jesus) the LORD of my life?

2. Is there unforgiveness or bitterness in my heart?

3. Am I involved, or have I been involved, with cults?

4. Am I involved in the occult or occult practices?

5. Am I now, or have I been in the past, involved in Satanism or witchcraft (of any kind)?

6. Have I done or spoken evil to a minister or rabbi of the Good News of Messiah?

If the answers to #2, #3, #4 or #5 above are "Yes," then:

1. **Pray to God and ask Him for forgiveness.**

2. **Renounce Satan.** Tell the devil that you no longer want anything to do with him or his works or workers.

Talk to the devil (renounce him) like this (command him):

"Satan, I renounce you and all your dark works and workers. In the name of Jesus, the Messiah of Israel, who defeated you with His BLOOD and RESURRECTION, I command you to leave me. I belong to the God of Israel. I take authority over you in the name of JESUS and cast you out of my life forever!"

Note: Use this same prayer for your family!

3. **Stay under the BLOOD of Mes**siah. If you can, find a good church or messianic synagogue which teaches the Good News Of Messiah and believes in healing and the gifts of the Holy Spirit. Read the Holy Bible and pray every day. Pray in tongues much to help build yourself up! Speak the BLOOD of Messiah over your life, your family, and your household (your belongings) every day.

4. Do NOT ally yourself closely with people who are involved in cults or the occult such as tarot cards, ouija boards, seances, or any psychic phenomena, new-age meditation, and the like. You are still to love them and communicate Messiah's (Christ's) Good News. Read in Deuteronomy 18:10-12 in the Torah to see what God thinks about this!

The Bible says, "The curse causeless shall not come." You do NOT have to worry if people try to put curses on you **if you know Messiah Yeshua (Jesus)!**

SELF DELIVERANCE

Through the years I have known cases of MIRACLES of deliverance which happened as a result of self deliverance. These were cases where the person suffered repeated defeat . . . as a Christian . . . in such areas as repeated sinful practice, lack of productivity, self depredation, or a false sense of inferiority. These were cases of sincere Christians who lived for the Lord, loved Him and feared Him, and who WANTED and KNEW they needed help.

These were also cases where the person KNEW how to pray for the deliverance of others. One day, years ago, the Lord revealed to me how to share with people like this the principle of self deliverance. It was amazing. I trust this teaching will help you to help others achieve the COMPLETE FREEDOM the Master purchased with His BLOOD!

This is a short, but very effective and useful method of deliverance. If this particular method does not pertain to you at this time, then keep it to have on hand so that you may access it in the future for someone who needs it.

I have known cases where people have been "bogged down" in sin, poverty, or repeated defeat, and have been instantly delivered through using the information described in this teaching.

You probably have never read the information contained in this teaching. The reason: lack of knowledge in this area.

Other than the Lord Jesus Christ, WHAT PERSON can pray for someone with such compassion and determination - and intimate knowledge of the problem(s) involved - than one's self?

Someone you know probably needs this message NOW. **Why not loan them this book to them after you are finished reading ... or purchase the book for them.** Think of someone you know who has had a repeated problem over a long period of time . . . or shorter, since having been born again . . . but has NOT received freedom from, or over, their problem.

The content of this teaching may be the answer for them; however, there are CONDITIONS that apply:

■ They must be a born again believer;

■ They must believe in The Deliverer, Messiah Jesus: and in His POWER and WILLINGNESS to deliver them;

■ They must know how to deliver others (even if they never have); and,

■ They must really want deliverance.

PREPARATION FOR DELIVERANCE

1. Develop a REASON, or a motive, for wanting deliverance. This is also something that can be reviewed, or reflected upon, from time to time to enforce the desire to remain free.

2. Read prayerfully scripture affirmations to build faith in God's Promises of deliverance. I have placed some that I have personally prepared in the **Addendum** of this book.

3. Know that deliverance is THE WILL of God

and is part of Christ's ministry. Jesus sent out his apostles to:

■ Preach and teach;

■ Heal; and,

■ Cast out demons.

If a person knows Jesus Christ as their Lord, NO demon, NO evil spirit can have them! Jesus said, *"If the Son therefore shall make you free, you shall be free indeed."* The Greek word here used for "indeed" [ontos] means "really, actually."

Deliverance belongs to the born again believer! To "**deliver**" is to "**set free**." Jesus said, ***"And you shall know the truth, and the truth shall make you free."*** [John 8:32]

Some people are bound by demons (spirits) of infirmity, or sickness. **Self deliverance may usually be effected in the same manner described below in the section "How To Minister Self Deliverance," especially with the "laying on of hands" being visualized in self deliverance.**

However, some cases are not resolved immediately because of "hindrances" to healing. These hindrances, as well as "gifts of healing" are covered fully in the unabridged book by Prince Handley titled: *Health and Healing*

Complete Guide to Wholeness. (Available at Amazon.com and other book distributors.)

There are also demon spirits which bind people financially, and in other areas of life. Good News: the BLOOD of Christ is effective in these areas, as in all areas, of life. In 2 Peter 1:4 we read that God has given to us "exceeding great and precious promises: that by these you may be partakers of the divine nature, having escaped the corruption that is in the world through lust."

One other solution that I have seen successful in problems of uncleanness or immorality -- the person has to really be serious and **know** what they're doing -- is for the person to **promise** God they will never take part in that practice, or habit, again.

"When you make a vow to God, defer not [put off or postpone] to pay it; for He has no pleasure in fools: pay that which you have vowed." [Ecclesiastes 5:4]

HOW TO MINISTER SELF DELIVERANCE

▪ See yourself in the midst of that problem.

▪ See yourself laying hands upon yourself, exorcizing [casting out] the demon spirit(s) that oppress you.

■ See yourself delivered from the problem.

SUGGESTION: You can also use the above to BLESS YOURSELF scripturally. That is, releasing the blessings of God in and upon yourself based upon scriptural truths and promises and with right motives: **1**. To build yourself up that you might serve the Lord more effectively; **2**. To edify the Body of Christ; and, **3**. To reach the world for Christ! Also, to be a blessing to your loved ones.

This is NOT a "mind game;" nor is it new age meditation or visualization. You are actually and literally ministering deliverance and blessing to yourself . . . IN FAITH . . . and through the power of the Holy Spirit. However, instead of praying for someone else, you're SEEING yourself in that place. It works! Real miracles result where Jesus the Messiah receives ALL the glory and His Kingdom is extended through holiness.

FREEDOM THAT LASTS

It's interesting to note that one of the names of the devil is "Beelzebub." The original Hebrew name means "Lord of the flies" and was the name of a Philistine god. It was a "dung god."

Have you ever considered what a title that Satan has: "Lord of the maggots, the manure god."

Dead blood draws flies. However, the GOOD NEWS is that the BLOOD of Jesus repulses Satan and his demons. Speak the BLOOD over your home and family. Just as the Israelites applied the BLOOD to their doors so that the death angel would pass over (see Exodus Chapter 12), so you can apply the BLOOD of Christ over your family and home by speaking it in faith over them.

Declare the BLOOD of Christ over your loved ones daily, as I mentioned above, and over all that God has given you by birth, adoption, or assignment: both NOW and in the FUTURE.

You will enjoy the presence of God as you praise God often throughout each day as a result of your deliverance. You will experience real freedom – freedom you can feel – and freedom that brings you JOY. "For the joy of the LORD is your strength." [Nehemiah 8:10]

YOUR FUTURE AND ETERNAL FREEDOM

In Isaiah 42:9 we read: **"Behold, the former things are come to pass, and new things do I declare: before they spring forth I tell you of them."** What a wonderful promise!

19

Let's examine what this passage is really showing us in the original Hebrew in which it was written. Let's see what the following words mean in the original language:

FORMER THINGS -- From the Hebrew **rishon** meaning **first (in place, time, or rank); ancestor, the ones before (in the times of the past); former things**.

PASS -- From a primitive root in the original Hebrew, the word **bo** means **to go or to come; to depart; fallen**.

NEW THINGS – **Chadash** means **fresh, or new thing**.

I -- Here used in Hebrew, **ani**, means not only **I**, but **I, myself**.

DECLARE -- The Hebrew word **nagad** means **to stand boldly out opposite; to manifest; to announce to one present**.

BEFORE -- **Tehrem** means **to interrupt or suspend** or **to make something or someone a non-occurrence**.

SPRING FORTH -- The word in the original **tsamach** means **to sprout, bud, (cause to) spring up or grow**.

TELL -- A primitive root in the Hebrew **shama**

20

meaning **to hear intelligently, discern, or understand**, implying **telling with the purpose of causing to obey or pay attention**.

Here is Prince Handley's paraphrase from the original.

"Listen, previous things from the past, AND even those things concerning your ancestors, are fallen, and fresh new things, I, myself, will announce boldly. I, myself, will interrupt the past.

I will now suspend the previous things with this announcement and I do so before the new things begin to spring forth and to grow. I do this so that you may intelligently discern and understand the new."

SUMMARY OF ISAIAH 42:9

God has interrupted your past, even that received as a result of your birth line. Just as He has fulfilled His prophecies pertaining to Israel, so He has suspended the previously inherited influences of your birth line.

God is telling you TODAY that **NEW THINGS** He has decreed for you are coming to pass. He is doing this so that you may DISCERN and KNOW the fresh new things are a SURETY, and realize once again that He is YWHH—ADONAI—God, The LORD, of Israel.

MEMORIZE GOD'S PROMISES

"No weapon that is formed against you shall prosper; and every tongue that shall arise against you in judgment you shall condemn. This is the heritage of the servants of the Lord, and their righteousness is of me, says the Lord."
-- Isaiah 54:17

"I beheld Satan fall as lightning from heaven ... I give you power ... over all the power of the enemy; and nothing shall by any means hurt you." -- Luke 10:19 / Jesus)

"When the evening arrived, they brought to him [Jesus] many that were possessed with demons: and he cast out the spirits with his word, and healed all that were sick."
-- Matthew 8:17

If you feel you need someone to assist you with deliverance, pray and ask God to lead you to a spirit-filled church where you can find **real** Christians or a minister who believes in the Baptism of the Holy Spirit and can pray for your deliverance. **Remember, not all churches are POWER churches.** Make sure they believe:

The Holy Bible is God's Word in entirety.

Jesus was miraculously born of a virgin.

Jesus is God who came to earth in human flesh.

The baptism of the Holy Spirit is evidenced by the gifts of the Spirit, healing, or speaking in tongues.

Deliverance is possible by the laying on of hands.

Also, it is very important to build yourself up in God's word every day. Start your day with God's Holy Word. I made a promise to myself years ago: "No Bible ... No breakfast." To help you, I have included some BONUS material at the end of this book in the **Addendum**: Scripture affirmations that I personally have chosen for **you**!

CONCLUSION

What I have shared with you in this teaching is POWERFUL. I trust you will have many testimonies to share in the future of people who were helped with this. Let us know by email to: princehandley@gmail.com.

Baruch haba b'Shem Adonai.

Your friend,
Prince Handley

P.S. – Check out the **Addendum** following where I have provided you with BONUS information: Powerful scriptural affirmations to help you with **Healing** and **Deliverance.** Read these aloud – so you can hear them – as needed. You may want to record them and listen to them often. They will build your faith and fill you with power to help **you** ... and to help you help **others**, also.

ADDENDUM

SCRIPTURES FOR YOUR DELIVERANCE

THE DEVIL WANTS TO HURT YOU AND MAKE YOU SICK
The thief (Satan) comes ... to steal, and to kill, and to destroy.
John 10:10

YESHUA WANTS TO HELP YOU AND MAKE YOU WHOLE
I am come that they might have life ... abundantly.
John 10:10

YESHUA WILL GIVE YOU POWER OVER THE DEVIL
I give you power ... over all the power of the enemy.
Luke 10:19

CONTINUE TO TRUST ONLY MESSIAH AS YOUR LORD - TURN FROM SIN

Stop sinning, so that nothing worse may happen to you.

John 5:14

DO NOT RECEIVE SICKNESS OR PAIN

Resist the devil, and he will flee from you.

James 4:7

RESIST SATAN AND HIS WORKS BY SPEAKING GOD'S WORD

Yeshua said unto him (the devil), 'It is written ...'

Matthew 4:1-11

SOME PEOPLE ARE BOUND BY A DEMON SPIRIT OF INFIRMITY

Cast out the spirits with a word.

Luke 13:11-13 / Mark 9:25 / Matthew 8:16

DEMONS AND SICKNESS ARE SUBJECT TO THE NAME OF YESHUA

Lord, even the demons are subject (submit) to us in your name.

Luke 10:17

THE NAME YESHUA IS ABOVE THE NAMES OF SICKNESS OR PAIN

God exalted him and gave him a name above every name.

Philippians 2:9

COMMAND SICKNESS OR PAIN TO 'GO AWAY' IN YESHUA'S NAME

Whoever shall say and not doubt ... shall have what he says.

Mark 11:23

YOU DO NOT HAVE TO TAKE SICKNESS OR DISEASE OR PAIN

He (Yeshua) took our infirmities, and carried away our diseases.
Matthew 8:17

YOU CAN BE HEALED BY SAYING GOD'S WORD AND BELIEVING IT

Confess with your mouth … and believe in your heart.
Romans 10:9

YOU CAN BE HEALED BY HEARING OR READING GOD'S WORD

He sent his word and healed them.
Psalm 107:20

YOU CAN BE HEALED BY HANDS LAID ON YOU IN JESUS' NAME

(Believers) shall lay hands on the sick, and they shall recover.
Mark 16:18

YOU CAN BE HEALED BY THE ANOINTING WITH OIL

Is any(one) sick? … call for the elders of the church.
James 5:14-15

YOU CAN BE HEALED IN BODY, MIND, AND SPIRIT

Heal me, O Lord, and I shall be healed.
Jeremiah 17:14

YOU CAN BE HEALED BY PROPER MENTAL ATTITUDE & PRAYER

All things are possible to him that believes.
Mark 9:23

YOU CAN BE HEALED BY A PRAYER CLOTH PLACED ON YOUR BODY
The diseases left them, and the evil spirits went out of them.
Acts 19:11-12

HEALING AFFIRMATIONS

GOD CREATED THE FIRST MAN NAMED ADAM
So God created man in his own image.
Genesis 1:27

THE DEVIL LIED TO ADAM CAUSING HIM TO DISOBEY GOD
And the serpent said ... You shall not surely die.
Genesis 3:4

ADAM DISOBEYED GOD, BRINGING SIN AND DEATH TO ALL MEN
By one man sin entered into the world, and death by sin.
Romans 5:12

PHYSICAL DEATH AND SICKNESS ARE THE RESULT OF SIN
Death passed upon all men, for all have sinned.
Romans 5:12

SIN SEPARATED MAN FROM GOD'S HEALTH AND LIFE
For all have sinned and come short of the glory of

God.
Romans 3:23

GOD'S SON, YESHUA HA MASHIACH, CAME TO EARTH TO HEAL THE SEPARATION

The reason (He) appeared was to destroy the works of the devil.
1 John 3:8

GOD'S SON WAS BEATEN, NAILED TO A CROSS STAKE FOR YOU

For God so loved the world, that he gave his only ... Son:
John 3:16

GOD SENT HIS SON TO EARTH AS PAYMENT FOR YOUR SINS

The LORD has laid on him the sin of us all.
Isaiah 53:6

ON THE CROSS STAKE YESHUA TOOK YOUR SICKNESS, DISEASE, AND PAIN

He has borne our sicknesses and diseases, and carried our pains.
Isaiah 53:4

HIS BODY WAS PUNISHED ... HIS BLOOD PAID THE PRICE: FOR HEALING

With his stripes (bruises) we are healed.
Isaiah 53:5

GOD RAISED HIS SON FROM THE DEAD ... HE IS ALIVE TO HEAL YOU

Messiah died for our sins ... was buried ... rose again.
2 Corinthians 15:3-4

YESHUA, THE ANOINTED ONE, NEVER REFUSED HEALING TO ANYONE

Yeshua went about ... healing all that were oppressed of the devil.
Acts 10:38

MESHIACH YESHUA'S HEALING NATURE NEVER CHANGES

Yeshua, the Messiah, the same yesterday, and today, and forever.
Hebrews 13:8

GOD PROMISES HEALING AND FORGIVENESS OF SINS TO YOU

Who forgives all your sins: who heals all your diseases. **Psalm 103:3**

GOD WANTS TO HEAL YOU - TO SAVE YOU FROM DISEASE AND SIN

I am the LORD that heals you.
Exodus 15:26

GOD WILL HEAL YOU AND KEEP YOU HEALTHY IF YOU SERVE HIM

You shall serve the LORD ... and I will take sickness away.
Exodus 23:25

ASK THE LORD YESHUA TO HEAL YOU NOW - ASK HIM TO SAVE YOU

Call upon me in the day of trouble: I will deliver you.
Psalm 50:15

LIVE A LIFE OF EXCELLENCE

For a complete work on health and healing:
***Health and Healing Complete Guide to
Wholeness***
by Prince Handley

Email requests to: princehandley@gmail.com

UNIVERSITY OF EXCELLENCE PRESS
Los Angeles ■ London ■ Tel Aviv

See next page for ***Other Books*** by Prince Handley

OTHER BOOKS BY PRINCE HANDLEY

- Map of the End Times
- How to Do Great Works
- Flow Chart of Revelation
- Action Keys for Success
- Health and Healing Complete Guide to Wholeness
- Prophetic Calendar for Israel & the Nations: Thru 2023
- Healing Deliverance
- How to Receive God's Power with Gifts of the Spirit
- Healing for Mental and Physical Abuse
- Victory Over Opposition and Resistance
- Healing of Emotional Wounds
- How to Be Healed and Live in Divine Health
- Healing from Fear, Shame and Anger
- How to Receive Healing and Bring Healing to Others
- New Global Strategy: Enabling Missions
- The Art of Christian Warfare
- Success Cycles and Secrets
- New Testament Bible Studies (A Study Manual)
- Babylon the Bitch: Enemy of Israel

AVAILABLE AT AMAZON AND OTHER BOOK STORES

UNIVERSITY OF EXCELLENCE PRESS